How to Raise a Puppy

A Child's Book of Pet Care

by Sara Bonnett Stein
photographs by Robert Weinreb

Random House   New York

Created by The Open Family Press/Media Projects Incorporated. Design by Mary Gale Moyes.

The author wishes to thank the Norwalk Veterinary Hospital, Norwalk, Connecticut, for its help in preparing this book.

Library of Congress Cataloging in Publication Data

Stein, Sara Bonnett. How to raise a puppy. (A Child's book of pet care) Includes index. SUMMARY: An easy-to-read guide to raising a puppy including discussions on selection, feeding, grooming, and training. 1. Dogs—Juvenile literature. 2. Animals, Infancy of—Juvenile literature. [1. Dogs]   I. Title.   II. Title: Puppy. SF426.5.S73   636.7'08'3   76-8137   ISBN 0-394-83223-X   ISBN 0-394-93223-4 lib. bdg.

Manufactured in the United States of America   2 3 4 5 6 7 8 9 0

Table of Contents

A Note to Parents

When parents get a puppy for a child, they envision a partnership. They hope the care the child gives and the love the dog returns will help both in their growing up. It's easier for children to form a partnership with a puppy they have chosen. If you have not yet given your child a puppy, find out what kind of dog he or she would like. That doesn't mean you have to buy a poodle that will bankrupt you at the grooming parlor. But if your child is hoping for a fluffy, funny dog, a fuzzy mutt might do.

The puppies shown in this book are a compromise between children's wishes and family practicality. The cockerpoo (a mongrel that is half cocker spaniel, half poodle) is fuzzy but relatively inexpensive and easy to groom. The golden retriever cross—another mongrel—is a good all-around family dog. The wire-haired dachshund is a small dog, but he isn't fragile. The bouvier des Flandres (a Belgian cattle dog) is an excellent watchdog, but she is gentle with children and sheds very little.

Other purebreds that make good family dogs are the Airedale, Scottie, basset hound, pug, standard schnauzer, and springer spaniel. They are all hardy and reliable, easy to care for, and easy to train.

To find out more about different breeds, read the descriptions in a dog encyclopedia. Breed descriptions are quite accurate. Talk with friends, too. Experience is even more informative. And nothing quite equals seeing different breeds for yourself by either going to dog shows or visiting breeders.

If you decide on a purebred dog, buy it directly from a breeder, not from a pet store or "puppy mill." Purebred puppies sold in stores are quite often unhealthy or inferior animals. Write to the American Kennel Club, 51 Madison Avenue, New York, NY 10010, and ask for the name of the secretary of the breed club that interests you—the dachshund club, for instance. The secretary of each breed club can help you locate a puppy in your part of the country.

Most breeders give health guarantees for their pups. The guarantee allows you to return a pup within a week if your vet finds the dog is unhealthy or has a physical defect. Don't buy a purebred puppy without such a guarantee. If the breeder has not already registered the pup with the American Kennel Club, he will tell you how to do so. Registering the dog is necessary only if you plan to breed or show him.

If you prefer to buy a mongrel, avoid pounds and pet shops unless the people there can assure you the puppy has been raised by its mother for at least two months, handled by people, and caged for no more than a week. The critical period for socialization in dogs is between 6 and 14 weeks of age. The best-adjusted puppies have had contact with both people and other puppies during this period. A deprived puppy will not make a good family pet. The best source for mongrels is classified ads placed in local newspapers by individual families. Seeing puppies in their own home lets you judge what sort of care they have had.

The choice of sex in a puppy is a matter of preference. Many experienced dog owners favor a bitch for a house pet. Females tend to stay close to home and are gentler and more responsive to people. Males may wander, or fight, or be rougher and less sensitive in their behavior. A bitch, however, comes into heat every six months, attracting both male dogs and dog-fights. If you don't want to breed your bitch, you can have her spayed after the first heat. The operation does not affect the bitch's personality.

You don't have to match the size of a dog to the size of your home. Many of the largest breeds are by nature less active than the smallest ones. A large dog will be neither restless nor underfoot in a small apartment and can be exercised sufficiently in his daily walks.

Dogs that have soft, heavy coats, such as English sheepdogs, or woolly coats, such as poodles, may need professional grooming. Keep coat in mind when choosing a breed if you want your child to be able to groom his dog himself.

For any dog to be a true family pet, he must live with the family. He can't live in a doghouse or be banished to the garage. The give-and-take of daily family life teaches a dog the friendliness and steadiness necessary with children. This doesn't mean you can't have a dog if you work and your child is at school all day. A dog can happily sleep his way through from morning to midafternoon by the time he is six months old. But the ideal time to get a puppy is at the beginning of the summer, when he will have several months of your child's company before school starts again.

Financially, any puppy is a luxury. The cost for a purebred dog can range from $75 to $500, but the most usual price is $150. Checkup, worming, and shots (including a rabies shot at six months) will cost between $30 and $80. Basic equipment—leash, collar, brush, food dish, and water dish—costs from $11 to $26. Chow and canned meat for the first year costs from $52 for a small puppy, such as a dachshund, to $145 for a larger puppy, such as a golden retriever. Spaying a bitch costs from $50 to $150, depending on the size of the dog. You will probably need a license when the puppy is six months old. The cost varies depending on where you live but is usually $3 for a male or a spayed female, more for an unspayed bitch.

Realistically, a puppy is a chore. There are many meals to feed, many puddles and bowel movements to clean up, much training to get done. Your child can't do it all by himself. Perhaps a five-year-old can feed the puppy breakfast but can't remember lunch and dinner, too. Perhaps an eight-year-old can clean a puddle but isn't thorough enough to clean up a bowel movement. Some eight-year-olds are persistent enough to train a dog to walk on a leash, but a five-year-old may lack the very strength it takes. And most children cannot give the constant attention needed to housetrain a dog. All the instructions for care and training in this book are addressed to children, but not in the expectation that they can take on all the chores. You and your child must decide together who can manage which jobs. There's work ahead for both of you.

No matter what arrangements you work out together, the puppy will still be a nuisance. He will chew socks, jump on guests, scatter garbage, and dig in the yard. A puppy's naughtiness is not your child's fault, and your child will not be good at stopping it. Children, especially those accustomed to hitting as a form of discipline, tend to strike out at puppies indiscriminately. Help your child understand that hitting a dog makes him scared of people, encourages him to do things behind your back rather than learn proper behavior, and may even make him bite back. A puppy pays more attention to an adult's discipline than to a child's, anyway. You decide on the rules. You do the scolding. It will work out better for the puppy—and for your child.

For all the cost, work, and annoyance, a puppy is still terrific fun. He will snuggle up, kiss ears, bounce, plop, gallop, and tumble. You would think there could be no problem here. A puppy's exuberance and a child's enthusiasm should make them perfect playmates. But a puppy may show affection by nibbling fingers, and his sharp baby teeth can hurt. A child can play vigorously for hours, but a puppy tires quickly. Becoming friends may not be a smooth process. To help, this book explains to your child about puppy cuddling and puppy play, puppy toys and puppy tricks.

At first, even if a child is as old as ten or eleven, he believes his puppy is like himself. He is sure the puppy agrees with what he is saying. He assumes the puppy enjoys what he enjoys. He is convinced the puppy shares his feelings, too. Without disillusioning your child of these beliefs, the information in this book, and some experience, will make him sensitive to the dog's feelings and preferences. From this learning grows a bond between a child and his dog. They have an understanding, those two. They are on the same side. They love each other.

Right now, your child and his puppy are very together. They will bumble about, both of them. In time your child will grow skilled; his puppy will have. You will see what you envisioned: your child and his dog growing up together.

Chapter One
A New Puppy

Getting a puppy is a wish come true. Here is your own puppy at last, as cute and cuddly as you pictured him. You can't keep your hands off his squirmy body. You can't keep your face from his fuzzy fur. You want to play with him all the time. You want to take him to bed with you. But your puppy has ideas of his own. He walks away from you. He makes a puddle on the floor. That's what wishes are like. They never come true exactly the way you pictured.

Taking care of a puppy is harder than promising to. It isn't hard to feed a puppy a meal. But it is hard to remember to feed a puppy three or four times every day. Taking care of a puppy is so much work that you will need help.

This book will tell you how to do all the jobs—feeding, brushing, bathing, cleaning up when your puppy goes to the bathroom on the floor, taking him outdoors, and training. Try each job. Figure out which ones you can do. Figure out which jobs you need help with. Parents don't mind helping if you are working, too.

Choosing a Puppy

When your parents say you can have a puppy, you probably can't wait till you get one. You want the puppy in the pet store window. You want the puppy the neighbors are giving away. Slow down! The puppy you choose now will be your dog for years. Take your time choosing him. Looking at puppies and thinking about them is fun, too.

Think about your puppy first. Close your eyes. Look at the pictures in your mind. Maybe you see a picture of a floppy puppy asleep in your arms. Maybe you see a picture of a big dog that growls at people you don't like. Or maybe you see a picture of a dog who can do tricks. The pictures are wishes. It

The puppies featured in this book are (from left to right across the spread): a cockerpoo, a golden retriever cross, a bouvier, and a wire-haired dachshund. The three smaller dogs are between two and three months old. The bouvier is five months old.

would be nice if the puppy you get is like your wish.

A basset hound is sleepy and floppy. An Airedale will try to protect you. A poodle likes to do tricks. And a mutt whose father or mother is a poodle might like to do tricks, too. Each kind of dog has its own kind of personality. A mutt that is mostly one kind of dog may have that personality, too.

Talk to friends who have dogs. That is a good way to find out what different kinds of dogs are like. Get books about dogs out of the library. The whole family can look at the pictures together. Talking together and looking at pictures can help you explain what kind of dog you are wishing for.

When you go to look at puppies, you may see one that you think is wonderful. But he might grow up to be awful.

You might love the littlest puppy, the runt of a litter. He is sad. He acts scared. He makes you feel so sorry for him. That kind of puppy can grow up still feeling sad and scared. He can stay too shy to be fun. He may snap at people with his teeth when he feels frightened.

You might love the most excited puppy. He squirms all over you. He licks your face. He rolls over, belly up. He seems to love you wildly. That kind of puppy can grow up still wild. He pulls at his leash. He jumps on people. He is wild all the time, and no one can stop him.

You might love the puppy that barks and whines at you. He seems to be talking to you. That kind of puppy can grow up noisy. The barking and whining don't go away. Nothing will keep him quiet.

These puppies all have problems. They are all worried or nervous or sad. Sometimes they have a problem because they have been in a pet store or in the pound for too long. They have not had enough love from people. Sometimes they have a problem because they were taken away too soon from their mother and the other puppies they were born with. They have not had enough company from other dogs. You can't cure these problems.

You need a happy puppy. A happy puppy has lived with

his mother and brothers and sisters for two months or even more. He has snuggled and romped with them all that time. A happy puppy has lived with a family of people. The people have cuddled him and played with him all that time, too. He has had the dog love and the people love he needs.

Try this when you look at puppies: Sit down on the floor. Notice which pups come to see you. They are the friendly ones. Pet them. Notice which ones stay on their feet, or walk into your lap without squirming or falling onto their backs. They are calm. Slap your hand down hard on the floor. The noise will startle the puppies and make them run off or back away. Notice which ones come back to see what the noise was. They are curious. Make a sudden movement toward the puppies. Notice which ones stay near you. They are brave. A good puppy for you is one that is friendly, calm, curious, and brave.

These wire-haired dachshund puppies are less than two weeks old. They are about six inches long.

Getting Ready

Before you bring your puppy home, you have to buy him a food dish, a water dish, a slip collar, and a leash. These are sold in pet stores and pet departments. You have to buy your puppy's food at a grocery store. And you have to make him a bed, and a place of his own to stay in at home.

Buy a food dish bigger than the puppy needs. Then you won't have to buy another when his meals get bigger. A dog who will be the size of a cocker spaniel needs a dish six or seven inches across. Bigger dogs need a ten-inch dish. Both the food dish and water dish should be heavy, so they won't tip over when the pup steps on the edge. Buy a bag of puppy chow and a few cans of chopped meat. (Pages 18 to 21 explain about food.)

A puppy wears a slip collar when he is on his leash. The slip collar is a piece of chain or cord with a ring at each end. The collar can be too big for your pup, too. It won't fall off him because the leash pulls it tight. Your dog should never wear a slip collar when he is loose by himself. A ring can get caught on something and choke him. (Page 40 tells how to put on the collar.)

The leash you buy should be flat, not round. A flat leash made of leather or cloth webbing is the easiest to hold. Some people also buy a chain leash. You can't walk a puppy on a chain leash because the chain will hurt your hands. But you can use it indoors when you have to tie up your puppy. He might chew through a leather leash, but he can't chew through chain.

At pet stores you can buy a tag that tells your puppy's name and address in case he gets lost. Buy a regular leather collar to attach it to. But wait until you can bring your puppy into the store to try on collars.

When he is six months old, your puppy will need two other tags. One is a dog license tag that you buy from your town. It has a number on it that belongs to your dog alone. The other tag is a rabies tag. An animal doctor gives you this tag when your dog gets a rabies shot.

A puppy who is going to be a pet should not live outdoors in a doghouse. A puppy needs to live with a family so he can learn what people are like and how they want him to behave. But your puppy will need a place of his own inside your home.

Make the puppy a bed out of a cardboard box. Ask your parents to cut down one side so the pup can climb out by himself. Put an old towel in the bottom to make his bed soft. If you are getting a very big puppy, a towel alone can be his bed. Make sure you have plenty of newspapers in your home. Newspapers will be your puppy's bathroom for a few months.

Decide on a place to keep the bed, the newspapers, and the water dish. Your puppy has to stay in that place when he is sleeping. He has to stay there when you are too busy to watch him, and when no one is at home.

One place to keep the bed is in a bathroom. You can close the door so the pup can't come out. Put bottles and brushes up high so he can't chew on them. Another good place is inside an old playpen. The puppy can't get out of it. And he won't be as lonely as he would be in the bathroom, because you can keep the playpen near you.

A corner of the kitchen is a good place for the puppy's bed, too. The floor is easy to clean, and the family is often in the kitchen to keep the pup company. He will have to be tied there with a leash so he can't wander off his newspapers. Choose a corner away from furniture. Put a hook into the wall three feet above the floor and hang the leash from it. Then the pup won't get tangled in his leash.

When you have chosen a place for your puppy, put his bed in a corner of it. Spread newspapers all around the bed, three sheets deep. In the bathroom, the newspapers should reach all the way to the door. They should cover the whole floor of the playpen. In the kitchen, they should come as far as the leash will reach. Put the puppy's water dish near his bed. You can keep his food dish there, too, if you want.

Now you have bought your puppy everything he needs and made his own place ready for him. It's time to bring him home. You can hold him in your arms or put him in a cardboard box. If you are bringing the pup home in a car, he may get carsick. Take paper towels with you for cleaning up, and a plastic bag to put dirty towels into. Spread newspapers on the floor of the car so the puppy can go to the bathroom there. For a long ride in hot weather, take a bottle of water and a dish so you can offer your puppy a drink.

Soon after you bring your pup home, he will have to get a checkup. The animal doctor will want to know certain things about him. When you pick up your puppy, ask the owner when the puppy was born. Ask if he has had any shots, and if he has, what kind and when. Ask what kind of food he has been eating, too. Write down the answers to your questions and keep them in a safe place.

The First Few Days

You have been waiting and wishing to be with your puppy. You have probably named him already. You are so happy when you bring him home. But your puppy may not be happy. He can't imagine how nice it will be to live with you. He misses the home he has lived in all his life. So he hides from you. Or he trembles and whines.

Feel very sorry for your puppy. As soon as you bring him home, carry him to his bed. (Page 30 tells how to carry a puppy without hurting him.) Lie down next to him. Talk to him softly. Say his name over and over. He will learn it in a few days if you say it often now. Smooth his fur slowly and gently. Talking and petting will make him feel better.

Fill the puppy's water dish. He may be thirsty. Make him a small meal. (Pages 18 to 19 tell you how.) Eating may make your puppy feel better. But if your puppy won't eat at first, don't worry. Throw out the food and try again later. Puppies don't starve themselves to death. In a day or two your puppy will feel hungry. Then he will eat.

On the first day, you'll have less work to do if you stay with your puppy in his own place most of the time. He will go to the bathroom a lot. Puddles and piles are easier to clean up when they are on the newspaper in the pup's place. (Pages 24 to 25 tell you how to clean up.)

Your puppy will be most unhappy when it is bedtime. Many puppies whine for the first few nights in their new home. The bed you made will help your puppy sleep. He feels safe in the cardboard box. He likes the soft towel. You can put a hot-water bottle under the towel to keep him warm. You can put a ticking wind-up clock under the towel, too. The ticking sounds like the mother dog's heart beating. The sound comforts the puppy. You won't need the hot-water bottle or the clock for more than a week.

Some people let the puppy sleep in his own place even if he whines. Other people can't stand the whining. They move the box and newspapers next to their own bed. When the

puppy cries, they can reach down and pet him. Your family can decide together whether your puppy should sleep in your room.

For the first few days, your puppy might be so upset that he gets diarrhea. If he does, feed him a mixture of cooked rice and cooked hamburger instead of dog food. If that doesn't help, your parents should call an animal doctor.

When a puppy is upset, he may roll onto his back when you come near. He lets out a few drops of urine. Puppies do this to protect themselves. In dog language it means, ''Don't hurt me. I'm only a baby.'' If your puppy behaves this way, don't play with him yet. Don't grab at him. He thinks you mean to hurt him, and he gives the puppy urine signal to keep himself safe.

In another day or two, your puppy will feel fine. He will put his ears forward when you call his name. He will start to play. He will jump on everyone and chew up everything. You don't have to feel sorry for him any more. Now you have to learn to take care of him, and he has to learn to be the kind of dog you want.

Going to the Vet

An animal doctor is called a veterinarian. The nickname is vet. Your puppy should go to the vet for a checkup during the first week you have him.

The vet will ask how old your puppy is, what kind of shots he has had, and when he had them. These are questions you asked the pup's owner. Bring the piece of paper with the answers when you go to the vet.

Also bring a spoonful of your puppy's bowel movement in a medicine bottle or plastic sandwich bag. The vet will call it a "stool sample." She will look at it through a microscope to see if your puppy has worms inside him. Many puppies do. The worms can make a puppy sick.

If your puppy is small, you can carry him into the vet's office. A big puppy can walk in on his leash. You will be in the waiting room with other people. Their dogs or cats may be sick. They feel worried, and their animals do, too. They don't want your puppy to visit them. Sit down. Hold your

puppy next to you.

When it's your turn, the vet will check your puppy on an examining table. You can lift your dog onto the table and help hold him still. The vet listens to the pup's heart with a stethoscope. She feels his belly to see if everything is fine inside. Then she looks at the puppy's teeth and in his eyes and ears. She pushes on his rear end to see how strong his legs are, and feels his bones to see that they are straight. She also checks his skin for rashes.

Afterwards, she will probably give your puppy a shot in the loose skin between his shoulders. The needle is small. The shot is quick. Most puppies don't notice it. The shot is very important. It keeps your puppy from catching three diseases: leptospirosis, distemper, and hepatitis. There is another kind of shot that your puppy must get when he is six months old. It keeps him from catching a disease called rabies.

If your pup has worms, the vet will give him a medicine. The medicine kills the worms. They come out of his body in diarrhea. Most families don't want to bother with the mess. Your puppy can stay with the vet for a few hours. Then you can take him home again. Stores sell worm medicines, too, but these are not safe to use without a vet's advice.

Before you leave, tell the vet what kind of food you are feeding your puppy, and what kind of food he had before you got him. Your vet may feel your puppy would be healthier with a different kind of food.

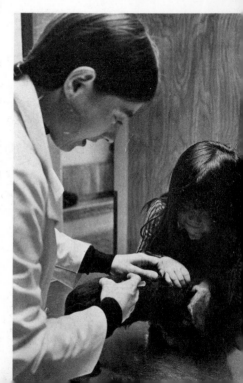

You may have some other questions that you want answers to. You wonder how big your puppy will be when he grows up. Or you are worried because your puppy threw up yesterday. You can ask any question. Vets don't think children's questions are silly. They will answer you seriously.

If the vet feels that there is a problem with your puppy, she may ask you to come back again or to call her. She will also tell you if your puppy needs a booster shot. Most vets will tell you when to bring your puppy back for a shot or a checkup. If no one does, ask—and write the answer down.

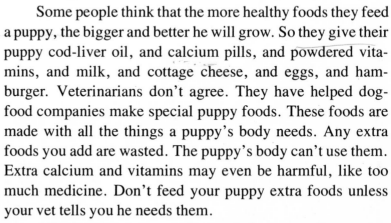

Chapter Two
Caring for Your Puppy

Feeding

Some people think that the more healthy foods they feed a puppy, the bigger and better he will grow. So they give their puppy cod-liver oil, and calcium pills, and powdered vitamins, and milk, and cottage cheese, and eggs, and hamburger. Veterinarians don't agree. They have helped dog-food companies make special puppy foods. These foods are made with all the things a puppy's body needs. Any extra foods you add are wasted. The puppy's body can't use them. Extra calcium and vitamins may even be harmful, like too much medicine. Don't feed your puppy extra foods unless your vet tells you he needs them.

All a healthy puppy really needs is puppy chow moistened with water. Chow is dry chunks of food. Chow cleans a puppy's teeth as he chews it. When your dog is one and a half years old, you can switch him to dog chow, a food that is made for grown-up dogs.

Some puppies and dogs don't like to eat plain chow. You can add a spoonful or two of canned dog meat to the chow to make it taste better. Try a few kinds of meat to see which ones your puppy likes best. Keep an opened can in the refrigerator until you use it up.

All your puppy's meals can be the same. He doesn't need a different food for breakfast, lunch, and dinner. Mix the chow and meat with water, not milk. Puppy chow already has dried milk in it. Young puppies like soft food. Warm water makes the chow soft. Older puppies like to chew. By the time they are six months old, they want the chow crunchy. You will need to add only a little water then.

No one can tell you exactly how big each meal should be. Start with about a half cup of chow for a small puppy, or a cup for a bigger one. Then watch how much he eats. If he eats everything, make his next meal a little bigger. If he doesn't finish his meal, give him a smaller meal next time. When your puppy walks away from his dish, he doesn't want any more. Throw out any food that is left. Wash the dish with soap. Rinse it well.

Feed a two-month-old puppy four times a day. His stomach is still small. He can't eat a lot all at once. But he is growing fast. He needs a lot of meals. He needs breakfast, lunch, an afternoon snack, and dinner.

As a puppy grows, his stomach grows, too. His stomach can hold more food. He wants more food in his dish. But he doesn't have to eat so many times a day. One day he will refuse his lunch. Or he will walk away from his afternoon snack. Then you know he doesn't need that meal any more. One day he cleans his plate, but still he licks and chews his dish. Then you know he wants a larger meal each time.

A three-month-old puppy usually wants three meals a day instead of four. When he is six months old, a puppy wants two meals instead of three. Sometime between the age of nine months and one year, he starts needing only one meal a day.

Some puppies stay skinny even though they eat a lot. They run around so much that they don't get fat. A skinny puppy usually fills out when he is about one year old. Some

puppies do get fat. They always clean their dish. They never refuse a meal. A fat puppy is not healthy. You have to put a fat puppy on a diet. Make his meals smaller. Give him fewer meals, too.

Puppies love to chew on bones. But there is only one kind of bone that is safe. It is the shin bone from a cow. In stores, this kind of bone is called a soupbone or marrowbone. You can buy soupbones in the supermarket. Or a butcher might give one to you free. Whole bones don't get smelly. Cut-up bones do. If a bone has been cut up, boil it for ten minutes to prevent a bad smell.

Any other kind of bone is not safe. Chicken bones, chop bones, and steak bones all break into splinters. A splinter can get stuck in a puppy's throat or stomach. You would have to take him to the vet right away. Dogs have died from swallowing splinters.

A puppy needs to drink water often. Fill a dish with fresh water when you feed your puppy breakfast. Leave the dish in his place all day. Clean it at the end of the day and fill it with fresh water again for the night. A puppy should have water to drink whenever he wants it.

Going Outdoors

As soon as your puppy feels at home, start taking him outside. He needs to get used to going to the bathroom there. But he will still make many messes indoors. He is too young to know better. Later on, you will train him to always go to the bathroom outdoors.

Try to take your puppy outside when he wakes up from a nap or when he finishes a meal. Put him on his leash unless you live very far from cars or unless your yard has a fence around it. Puppies don't understand about moving cars. Many puppies have been hurt or killed by running out into the street. Pages 40 to 41 explain how to get your puppy used to a leash.

If you live in an apartment building, carry your puppy outdoors. If you don't carry him, he may go to the bathroom in the lobby or in the elevator.

Some puppies don't like to go out at first. Your puppy may hate the rain or the cold. He may be scared of strange smells and people. The puppy has to get used to these things. You can feel sorry for him, but he has to go out anyway.

Some puppies love to go outdoors. Your puppy may get so excited that all he wants to do is play. Don't play with him at first. Walk with him until he goes to the bathroom.

Puppies like to use grass for bathrooms. They also like places that other dogs have used. In the city or in a suburb, walk your puppy in the gutter where other dogs have been. Don't let your puppy make a pile on the sidewalk or on someone's lawn. In the country, walk your dog in grassy places. But don't let him make piles where people might step in them.

Watch your puppy. When he makes a puddle or a pile, pat him. Tell him he is good. Patting your puppy and praising him shows him he has done the right thing. When he has finished going to the bathroom, you can play and run with him.

Maybe you will meet other dogs outside. Your puppy may want to play with them. But he should not play with other dogs until he has had his first shot. Also, some dogs are nasty, even to puppies. If you don't know the other dog, ask his owner if your pup can play with him.

Cleaning Messes

Even though you take your puppy outside, he will make puddles and piles in your home for several months. Cleaning them up is hard. There may be a lot of them, and you won't like their smell. But cleaning up messes is part of caring for a puppy.

The mess your puppy makes on the newspapers near his bed is the easiest to clean. Fold up the dirty newspapers. Put them in a plastic garbage bag. Throw the bag in the outside garbage can, not the kitchen pail. Put fresh newspapers down.

When your puppy goes to the bathroom away from his newspapers, cleaning the mess is harder. Here is what you will need:

paper towels
a big floor sponge that is used only for this job
a two-cup measuring pitcher
white vinegar
clear ammonia
an old dustpan that isn't needed for other work
small plastic garbage bags

Soak up puddles on the bare floor with paper towels. Throw the wet towels in the kitchen garbage pail. Don't throw them in a wastebasket. They will smell. Wet the sponge. Wipe the floor where the puddle was. Then wash the sponge with detergent, rinse it, squeeze it out, and put it away.

If the puddle is on a rug, it can make a white stain that will never come out. The stain doesn't show at first. But it will show in a few weeks. First soak up the puddle with the paper towels. Then put a quarter cup of vinegar into the two-cup measuring pitcher. Fill up the pitcher the rest of the way with cold water. Pour enough vinegar-water over the damp spot to make it soaking wet. Let the spot stay wet for a few minutes. Then soak up the vinegar-water with more paper towels. The vinegar will keep the rug from staining.

When your puppy makes a bowel movement off his newspapers, pick up the pile with toilet paper. Flush the pile and the paper down the toilet. You may have to use a lot of toilet paper. That could clog the toilet. If the pile is very big, first pick up part of it and flush it away. Then pick up the rest and flush a second time. Wet the sponge and put a few drops of detergent on it. Scrub the spot where the pile was. Rinse the sponge and wipe the detergent off the floor or rug. Then rinse the sponge again.

If a puppy has diarrhea or if he throws up, the mess is too hard for you to clean up alone. You need an older person's help. The job calls for ammonia, which is a poison and can also hurt your eyes and skin.

Scrunch up some paper towels. Push a dustpan under the mess. Use the bunch of towels to push the mess onto the dustpan. Then push the towels and mess into a plastic garbage bag. Wipe up what is left on the floor with more paper towels. Put them in the garbage bag, too. Put the bag into the outside garbage can, not the kitchen pail. Wash the dustpan with detergent. Then wipe the floor again with a wet sponge and a few drops of ammonia. Ammonia takes out the smell.

If vomit or diarrhea is on a rug, pick it up with the paper towels and dustpan. Then mix a quarter cup of ammonia with cold water in the two-cup measuring pitcher. Pour the ammonia-water on the spot. Let it stay there for a few minutes. Then scrub the rug with a sponge, and wipe it with paper towels until it is clean and fairly dry.

Grooming

Brushing or combing a dog is called grooming. Groom your puppy when his hair gets tangled or dusty. Groom him to remove loose hairs. Dogs are always losing some hair. And when the weather is warm, or the heat is on indoors, they shed a lot of hair to keep cool.

Short-haired dogs, such as beagles, need only brushing. Brush them every few days when they are shedding a lot. Other dogs should be both brushed and combed. Woolly dogs, such as the cockerpoo on the next page, get awful tangles unless they are groomed every week. Long-haired dogs, such as cocker spaniels, need combing to remove tangles. They may need brushing only when they are shedding a lot.

You can buy dog brushes and combs at a pet shop. A dog comb is made of metal. There are three kinds of dog brushes. One kind is made of bristles like your own hairbrush. Use it on short-haired dogs. Another kind of brush has metal bristles. Use it on wire-haired dogs, such as Scotties. The third kind of brush is made of thin bent wires. It is called a slicker. Slickers are for dogs with woolly coats, or for any dog that gets many tangles.

At first your puppy won't like to be groomed. He may try to chew on your hand or on the brush and comb. If you try to groom him in your lap, he will squirm away from you. The best place to groom your puppy is on a table. He can't run away there. And he can see that grooming is serious. He has never played on tables.

Grooming is a two-person job. One person holds the puppy's head high with a leash. The other person brushes and combs. Loose hair will come out into the brush and comb. Before you start grooming, get a paper bag to put the hair into. Put the puppy's slip collar and leash on. Lift him onto the table. You may have to stand on a chair to hold the leash up straight.

Clockwise from top: A dog comb, a bristle brush, a slicker, and a metal-bristle brush

Start brushing or combing along your puppy's back and sides. That is where he will like it best. Clean out the brush or comb when it gets full of hair. Put the hair in the paper bag. Take out burrs by pulling apart the hairs around them. Cut out mats (solid tangles) with blunt scissors. Wash out sticky tangles with a wet sponge. When you get to your puppy's back legs, he will sit down to stop you. Holding one arm under his belly will make him stand still.

Your puppy won't like you to brush his tail, paws, ears, and face. Hold his head up high so he can't nip or jump off the table. Don't yell at him or slap him. Talk to him nicely so he knows that you are not trying to be mean. When he gets older, he will be more patient with grooming.

When you finish grooming, check your pup for ticks and fleas. The bites of these insects can make your puppy sick. And he may scratch himself until his skin is sore. Check the skin on his back, sides, and belly for bites and insects. Ticks look like small brown scabs. They bite into a dog's skin and fill up on his blood. Then they become lumps the size of your fingertip. Pull ticks out with your fingers. Ticks are hard to kill, so flush them down the toilet. Fleas are tiny black bugs that jump very quickly. They leave droppings that look like little black crumbs on your dog's skin.

You can kill fleas, and ticks too, with special sprays and powders. These are sold in pet stores. Follow the instructions on the package to spray your puppy and his bed. Don't use any other kind of insect killer. It could make your puppy sick. Don't use flea or tick collars either. Many dogs get a rash from wearing them.

Check your puppy's toenails when you groom him. If they touch the floor, they are too long and should be cut. If your puppy has dewclaws (an extra nail high up on each foot), check how long they are, too. Cutting toenails is hard to do without hurting your puppy. The vet can clip his nails the first time. And she can show your parents how to do it with special toenail clippers sold at pet stores.

Bathing

Most puppies don't need baths if they are brushed often enough. Too much bathing makes them itch. But if your puppy gets into something smelly, or if he looks dirty, or if your hands get dirty when you pet him, he needs a bath. First take him outside so he can go to the bathroom. It will be a few hours before he is dry enough to go out again.

It takes two people to bathe a puppy. One person holds him on a leash. The other washes him. Both people will get wet, so wear old clothes or put on a bathing suit.

Get ready three towels, a plastic pitcher, baby shampoo, and the puppy's slip collar and leash. Bathe a small puppy in the kitchen sink. You can sit on the counter to hold the leash. Bathe a big puppy in the bathtub. Sit on a rear corner of the tub, with your feet in the water, to hold the leash. A rubber mat on the tub bottom keeps puppies from slipping.

Fill the sink or tub with enough warm water to reach your dog's belly. If you are worried about getting shampoo in his eyes, put a drop of mineral oil or vegetable oil into each eye with an eye dropper. Put on the pup's slip collar and leash. Lift him into the water. Keep the collar just behind his ears. Hold his head away from the edge so he won't drip water on the floor. Pull the leash straight up. The puppy can't try to jump out of the bath if his head is held high. He can't move away either.

Dip the pitcher in the water and wet the puppy from the neck down. (Save the puppy's head to wash last.) Soap him all over with the baby shampoo. Lift his legs one at a time to soap his paws. Try not to make him slip. Don't rinse him yet.

Now comes his head. Dogs hate to have their faces washed. Hold tight to the leash. After the puppy's head is soaped, use the pitcher to rinse it with clean warm water from the tap. Dry his head with a towel, or he will shake it and get soap and water all over everything.

Let out the dirty water. Rinse the rest of the puppy with clean warm water from the tap. Use the pitcher, or a spray attachment if you have one. Feel the pup's belly and chest to be sure they are rinsed, too.

Your puppy will want to shake the water off himself right away. If you are washing your puppy in the sink, throw a towel over him and let him shake under that. If he is in the bathtub, pull the shower curtain closed so he can shake. Before you let him out, dry him as much as you can with towels. Then lift him out of the sink, or let him jump out of the tub.

The puppy still won't think he is dry enough. He will try to dry himself on the rugs and along the edges of furniture. But if you have rubbed him well with the towels, he won't be wet enough to hurt anything. Don't let him go outdoors for a few hours. He might get too cold. And he might roll in the dirt to dry himself.

Loving Your Puppy

People show they love each other by cuddling and playing. But you don't feel loved if someone cuddles you too roughly. You don't feel loved if someone plays in a scary way. People who love you have to be careful of your feelings.

When you love a puppy, you have to be careful of his feelings, too. You have to cuddle him the way he likes to be cuddled. You have to play the way he likes to play.

Some of the ways people play are not fun for puppies. You may like to hold hands and pull another child around, or hold someone's legs and play wheelbarrow. Puppies don't play this way. Their legs don't bend the way yours do. When you pull on them, they hurt. Holding onto a puppy's paw frightens him. Don't play wheelbarrow with your puppy. Don't hold his paws and swing him around. Don't pull him along the floor by his legs or paws. And don't pull his tail. That hurts!

There are other things your pup may not like. He may not like being carried around, or hugged hard, or dressed up, or pushed about in a baby carriage. When a dog is unhappy, his tail droops. His head droops, too. He may roll his eyes so you can see whites on the sides. He may try to get away from you. When you notice your puppy looking unhappy, stop what you are doing with him.

Puppies are like human babies. They get tired before you do. They sleep more than you do, too. When you play with your pup, stop after a while. Walk away from him and sit down. If your pup comes bouncing over to you, he wants to play some more. If he plops down, he wants to sleep. It is time to carry him to his bed.

If you pick up a puppy by holding him around his belly or under his front legs, he will feel miserable. It hurts him and he thinks he might fall. Here is how to carry a puppy so he feels safe and comfortable: Hold your arms like a cradle. One arm fits under the puppy's chest in front of his legs. The other

The right way to carry a dog

arm fits under his rear end behind his legs. If he is tiny, use your hands instead of your arms.

When you want to calm down a pup, cuddle him this way: Put your hand flat on the puppy's head just above his eyes. Stroke your hand back along his head and down his neck. Talk to him gently. Stroke him over and over again. He may like to be scratched, too—behind his ears, between his shoulders, along his neck, on his rear end, and on his chest. He may roll onto his back, belly up. Then he wants you to rub his belly.

Stroking, scratching, and rubbing are all calm ways to cuddle a puppy. There is an excited way, too. It is called patting. Patting is gentle slaps on a dog's side. Patting a dog is like saying "Hooray!" Your puppy will say "Hooray" back by wagging his tail and wiggling.

Puppy Games

Puppies play only a few kinds of games: "chase-and-pounce," "shake-it-dead," "chew-it-up," and "catch-me-if-you-can." When dogs were wild, these games taught puppies how to chase a rabbit, pounce on it, shake it dead, and chew it up for dinner. "Catch-me-if-you-can" taught puppies to run away from their enemies. Puppies use each other for make-believe rabbits and make-believe enemies. Your puppy will use you that way, too. He will chase you and pounce on you, tug on your clothes and yank your hair, and nip you and chew on you. He will run away so you can chase him.

At first these games are fun. But then they get rougher. The puppy bites harder. He tears your shirt. He chews up socks and shoes and table legs. He pounces so hard he knocks you down. When he runs away he is too fast to catch. Your pup has to learn to play his games with toys. He has to learn not to play "catch-me-if-you-can" at all.

"Chase-and-pounce" is played with a ball. Solid hard-rubber balls are the best. Puppies can't make holes in them or chew them up. When you play "chase-and-pounce" with your pup, you roll or throw the ball and your pup chases it. Sit still after you throw it. Don't try to grab the ball away from your puppy. He will learn to bring the ball back when he wants you to throw it again. If you run after him, he will think you are playing "catch-me-if-you-can." Don't ever play that game with your puppy. If you chase him, he will never learn to come to you.

Your puppy can play "shake-it-dead" with a knotted rag or a piece of rope. Or you can buy him special toys made of rubber or leather at pet stores. Hold the toy and drag it along the floor. When the puppy grabs it, let him tug on it and shake it back and forth.

The best toy for "chew-it-up" is made of rawhide. Pet stores and pet departments sell rawhide toys in different sizes

and shapes. Rawhide is made of animal skin. It gets soft and chewy in a puppy's mouth. It tastes good. When your puppy chews on things he is not supposed to, say "NO!" Give him a rawhide toy or a soupbone instead.

Even if your puppy plays with toys, he may still pretend you are a rabbit. A mother dog lets her puppies pounce on her and nip her for a while, just as we let babies act like babies. But when she has had enough, she snaps at the pups with her teeth. That stops them. You must let your puppy know when you have had enough, too. When he jumps on you, or nips you, or tugs your clothes, slap your hand right into his nose. Slap hard. Say "STOP!" You do not have to let your puppy hurt you.

Puppies misbehave in other ways. They chew on things they are not supposed to. They dig holes in the yard. They jump up on the furniture and get into the garbage. If you hit your puppy for all the mistakes he makes, he will get scared of you and of your hands. He may get so scared of being hit that he can't even remember what he did wrong. Hit your pup only when he does something that hurts you. When your pup is naughty in other ways, pull him away from what he is doing. Say "NO! BAD DOG!" Don't yell. Just use a firm, serious voice.

Teaching your puppy what is naughty takes a long time. You and your parents will have to work together to teach him. Sooner or later he will learn how you want him to behave.

Playing "chew-it-up" with a rawhide toy

A Sick Puppy

You may have heard that when a dog has a warm nose, it means he is sick. Or when he eats grass, it means he has worms. These stories are not true. Healthy dogs can have warm noses and eat grass. Healthy dogs also vomit easily. They vomit to get rid of things they have swallowed but can't digest. Warm noses, eating grass, and vomiting once in a while are not signs of sickness.

But puppies can get colds and rashes and cuts and ear infections, just as you can. If your puppy is hurt or sick, you can help to take care of him.

You spend a lot of time with your puppy. You may be the first one to notice when something is wrong. Something is wrong with your puppy's leg or paw if he starts to limp. Something is wrong with his ears if he scratches them or shakes his head a lot. Something is wrong with his skin if he scratches it all the time or if you feel scabs or see bald spots. And something is wrong inside your puppy's body if he acts very restless or very sad, if he won't play or eat, or if he throws up many times or coughs a lot. If you notice any of these things, tell your parents so they can call the vet.

The vet will check your puppy to see what is wrong. She will tell you what to do. She will give you the kind of medicine that will make him better. If your puppy is seriously sick, she will keep him in the animal hospital to take care of him.

Dogs don't like to take medicine. They may not stay quiet when they are supposed to. And they hate to have their temperature taken.

Hide pills inside a meatball. Make the meatball out of liverwurst or canned dog meat. Stick the pill into the middle. Your puppy will eat the meatball without noticing the pill.

Pour a dose of liquid medicine into a small bottle. Use exactly the amount your vet said to use. Ask someone to stand behind your puppy and hold his head up. Pull out his bottom lip near the corner of his mouth. Pour the medicine into the pocket his lip makes. Stroke your puppy's throat until he swallows the medicine.

Put ointment on a dog when he is sleepy. Stroke him for a while first. Talk gently to him. Then put the ointment on while he is feeling calm.

Take a puppy's temperature with a regular rectal thermometer while he is lying on his belly across your lap. Put vaseline on the thermometer first. Ask an older person to put the thermometer into his rectum. Hold the dog so he doesn't squirm around. Smooth his fur and talk to him quietly. The thermometer should stay in for two minutes. A puppy has a fever if the thermometer reads over 102° F.

Keep a sick puppy tied up on his leash if he is supposed to stay quiet. Fold up a blanket for him to lie down on. Spend as much time as you can sitting with him. Keeping a puppy company makes him feel better when he is sick.

A puppy gets a dose of liquid medicine (above) and has his temperature taken.

Chapter Three
Training Your Puppy

Housetraining

When you got your puppy, you chose a place in the house for his bed. You put newspapers by his bed to be his bathroom. Probably your puppy almost never messes in his bed. He walks away from it when he has to go to the bathroom. He goes on the papers if he can. He is already trying to be neat. And you have praised him when he went to the bathroom outside. He already knows that pleases you.

When dogs lived wild, they slept in dens. They didn't go to the bathroom inside their dens. They walked away from them and went outside. Your puppy's sleeping place is like a den. He walks "outside" it to make messes. But what is outside to him is still inside your home. He has to learn that your whole house is a den. He has to learn to always go outdoors to go to the bathroom. Teaching him that is called housetraining or housebreaking.

You can start housetraining your puppy when he is three months old. You housetrain a puppy by helping him to make piles and puddles outside, and by scolding him when he does it indoors. The job is hard. You have to watch the pup a lot. A three-month-old puppy can make two puddles every hour. He can make six piles every day. You will need your family's help to housetrain the pup.

Keep the puppy in his own place on his newspaper as much as you can. Take him outdoors after every meal. Puppies often make a pile after eating. Let him take his nap in his bed. When he wakes up, take him outdoors. Puppies always puddle after a nap. Keep your puppy in his bed at night. Try to get up early—as early as 6:30. Take your puppy out before he has to use his newspapers.

But a puppy can't be tied up or closed in all day long. He needs company and play. He needs to come out of his den. That's when he will mess in the house. First, he makes a sign. If you watch carefully, you will notice the signs a puppy makes before going to the bathroom.

He may stop playing and walk away. He holds his head low. He is about to puddle. He may start to circle about and sniff. He is about to make a pile. He may disappear behind a chair or go into another room. He is looking for a private place to make a mess.

Each time you see your puppy make a sign, say "Out?" Put on his slip collar and leash. Pick him up and take him outside. Wait until he goes to the bathroom. Then tell him he is wonderful. Pat him a lot.

Often you will not be in time. Your puppy will make a puddle or pile before you can get him outside. Don't yell. Don't spank him. Yelling and spanking scare a puppy so much that he can't think what he did wrong. Hold him by the skin on the back of the neck. Shake him. Say "BAD!" in a serious voice. Then take him outside.

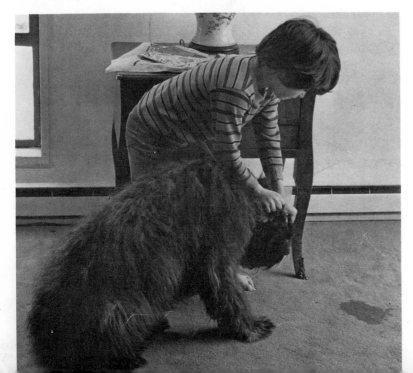

Shake a puppy when you catch him making a mess in the house.

If you find a mess long after your puppy has made it, don't scold him at all. He has forgotten about the mess. He won't know what you are scolding him for.

As a puppy gets to be four or five months old, he makes fewer messes. He can hold himself longer. He can wait until later in the morning. Sometimes he makes a pile in a secret place. He knows it is wrong. Sometimes he walks to the door before he puddles. He knows that is right. He is getting housetrained.

Help him learn. Take his newspapers away now. He shouldn't need them any more when he is four or five months old. But keep him in his own place when you can't watch him. Close doors to rooms so he can't mess in secret places. When he goes to the outside door, say "Out?" Then take him outside. Wait for him to go to the bathroom. Always pat him afterwards.

This puppy barks at the window next to the door when she wants to go outside.

Most dogs can be housetrained by the time they are five or six months old. They still have accidents, but they are sorry. Some dogs are especially hard to train. If your dog isn't housetrained by the age of six months, be patient and keep working with him. Watch him as much as you can. Your whole family should help.

It can take a long time to housetrain a puppy. But sooner or later, your puppy will learn to make a strong sign to tell you that he wants to go outside. A strong sign is scratching at the door, or barking or whining at the door. When your puppy learns to make a strong sign, he is housetrained.

Say "Good dog!" each time your puppy goes to the bathroom outdoors.

Making a loop in a slip collar

How a slip collar should look when you walk a dog on your right side (above) and your left side

Walking on a Leash

You have to teach your puppy to walk beside you on a leash. Otherwise the pup will pull you wherever he wants to go. He will hurt your arm and hand, or even pull you down. Then it will be too hard for you to walk him, and it won't be any fun to take him places.

Your puppy should wear a slip collar when you walk him on his leash. A dog's neck muscles are thick and strong. Your pup would not feel a regular collar much, even if you pulled hard on the leash. But a slip collar tightens quickly when you jerk on it. Then it feels very uncomfortable to your pup. He stops trying to pull away from you. The slip collar won't hurt him. It loosens again quickly.

To put on the slip collar, first make a loop in it. The first picture on this page shows you how. You take the middle of the chain or cord and drop it through one of the rings at either end. The chain forms a big loop under the ring. Put the loop over your puppy's head.

There is a right way and a wrong way to put on a slip collar. When the collar is on the right way, it slips loose after you jerk on it. When the collar is on the wrong way, it sticks and doesn't loosen. Then the puppy chokes.

The second picture on this page shows how to put the collar on if you want your dog to walk on your right side. The third one shows how to put it on if you want to walk your dog on your left side. Decide which side you find most comfortable. Then put the collar on the way that the picture shows. Putting on the collar is confusing at first. You may need help.

When the collar is on, attach the leash to the ring that hangs free. Now you are ready to walk your dog.

Puppies act silly when you first try to walk them. When you tug on the leash, they sit down and won't move. Sometimes they buck like horses. Don't try to drag your puppy along. Squat down. Call him in a high, happy voice. Use his name. Give the leash a little tug. Keep encouraging him with gentle tugs and a cheery voice. He will get used to the leash and begin to walk with you.

As soon as the puppy walks with you, you can start teaching him to walk without pulling. You do it by jerking the leash whenever the pup pulls away from you.

Hold the leash so it is a little loose. Start to walk. If the puppy lags behind you, jerk the leash forward very fast, then quickly let it loose again. Do it again and again until your pup catches up with you. Pat him and say ''Good pup!''

If the puppy rushes ahead of you, jerk the leash back, then quickly let it loose again. Do it again and again until your pup slows down. Pat him some more.

With each jerk, the collar tightens suddenly, then slips loose again. The pup lags behind . . . SCRUNCH! the collar tightens. He runs ahead . . . SCRUNCH! the collar tightens. He is comfortable only when he walks next to you.

Teaching "sit"

Teaching "lie down"

Learning Words

Dogs wag their tails when they see you are happy. They lick your face when you cry. They seem to understand your feelings. But dogs don't understand your words unless you teach them to. The first word a puppy learns is his own name. He learns it because you say it so many times, and because it is always the same word.

When you teach a pup a new word, you have to say the same word every time. You can't say "Come" one time, and "Get over here" the next time. Dogs are not that smart. They can't figure out that all those words mean the same thing. You can't hide the word in a lot of other words either. You can't say "I told you to sit and I mean it." Your dog won't be able to hear "sit" mixed up with the other words. You have to say any new word many times, just as you said your puppy's name.

Puppies are very different from one another. One puppy will learn a new word in one day. Another puppy won't learn it for weeks. But almost all puppies learn best if you teach them for just a few minutes at a time, several times a day.

The words that are easiest to teach are "sit" and "lie down." You teach the word by saying it, then making the puppy do it, then telling him he is a good pup. Here is how to teach your puppy "sit": Hold one hand on his neck—or pull his leash up—so he can't walk away. Say "SIT!" Push down on his rear end with your other hand to make him sit down. Tell him he is great even if he sits for only a second.

"Lie down" is harder to teach than "sit." You can't push a dog to make him lie down. His legs are too strong. Make your puppy sit first. Then say "LIE DOWN!" Gently lift his front paws with both your hands. Slide his paws forward until he is lying down. Then tell him how good he is. If your puppy struggles when you hold his paws, move your hands farther up his legs.

After your puppy has learned to sit, you can teach the

word "stay." But "stay" is harder for a puppy to learn, and will take longer. Tell your puppy to sit. Hold your hand in front of his nose. Say "STAY!" when he gets up. Slap your hand gently into his nose. Make him sit again just where he was. Try again. Say "STAY!" Gently slap his nose every time he moves. When he does stay, don't make a big fuss over him or he will get up again. In a calm voice, tell him he is a good dog.

When your pup learns to stay with you right next to him, try walking backwards away from him. If he follows, be ready to stop him. He has to learn that "STAY!" means stay, even when you walk away. He can learn to stay when he is lying down, too.

Teaching "stay"

"Come" is hard to teach. Puppies don't always like to come when they are told to. And sometimes people confuse their pup by chasing or scolding or spanking him when they tell him "Come." The pup learns that "come" means something bad. He stays away when he hears the word.

Call "COME!" to your puppy when he is running to you anyway. Then tell him he is wonderful. Say "COME!" when you have him on the leash. Then pull him right up to you and tell him how smart he is. When you are playing with your puppy, say "COME!" in a high, cute voice. Squat down. Clap your hands. Make a big fuss when he comes to you. You have to make coming to you more fun than anything else your puppy is doing.

Teaching "come"

Sit, lie down, stay, and come are useful words. They are words that will help your dog to behave well. As your dog begins to learn each word, use it a lot.

If you want to go out, but you don't want your dog to follow you, say "STAY!" If he is bothering the family at dinnertime, tell him to lie down. If he is in the way in a store, make him sit. People will be pleased with your well-behaved puppy. You will be proud of him. And he will be proud of himself.

Learning Tricks

Some puppies bat at you with one paw when they want you to pet them. If you say "SHAKE HANDS" and the paw lands in your hand, that is a trick. Some puppies bark to make you hurry with their dinner. If you say "SAY PLEASE," and then the puppy barks, that is a trick, too. Some puppies stand on their hind legs to sniff their dinner as you fix it. If you say "DANCE," and then the puppy stands up, that is another trick. Tricks can start with something the puppy does by himself. Then you teach him the word for what he is doing. He learns to do the trick whenever you say the word.

If a puppy never barks for his dinner, it is hard to teach him "say please." Find a trick that your puppy already does in some way. Then all you have to do is teach the word for it.

Practice tricks whenever you feel like it. Some puppies learn a trick right away. Others take a long time. If you get mad when your puppy doesn't learn something quickly, he will feel unhappy. Then he won't want to learn at all. You have to be kind and patient. You have to be sure your puppy is having a good time.

One way to be sure a puppy is having a good time is to give him food. Dogs like to do tricks to get food. Use puppy chow, dog biscuits, or bits of cheese or lunch meat. Hold the bit of food in your fist. The puppy can smell it, but he can't grab it from you.

To teach your pup to dance, hold your fist above his nose so he can smell the food. Say "DANCE." When your puppy stands up to sniff the food, hold your fist just above his nose to keep him standing. Then give him the food. Don't hold your fist too high or he will jump for the food and plop down again. When your puppy learns to stay standing for a longer time, you can move your fist in a circle. He will learn to turn around on his hind legs to follow your fist. That's how he will dance.

"Shake hands"

"Say please"

If you want your puppy to say please, hold the food in your fist. But this time sit down so your puppy doesn't dance or jump. Tell him "SAY PLEASE." Use a very excited voice. You can even bark to give him the idea. When he barks once, give him the food before he barks any more.

You don't have to use any food to teach your puppy to shake hands. When your puppy is sitting in front of you, pet him a little. Then stop. Say "SHAKE HANDS" and hold your hand ready. He may paw you to remind you that you were petting him. Catch his paw and shake it once. Don't squeeze it. Then pet him some more. If your puppy doesn't paw at you, tap the back of his leg. Tapping usually makes a dog lift his paw.

Growing Up

As your puppy grows, his body changes. So does the way he acts. A male dog starts to lift his hind leg instead of squatting to make a puddle. He likes to sniff around female dogs, but he may try to fight with other males. Now he is getting old enough to mate with females and make puppies. He may try to practice mating by grabbing other dogs with his front paws and holding onto them. He may even grab your leg and hold on when he is playing with you.

If your puppy is a female, her body changes, too. One day when she is seven or eight months old, you may notice a few drops of blood coming from her rear end. There is nothing wrong with your puppy. The bleeding is called "coming into heat." It is a sign that your puppy is growing up. She is getting old enough to mate with males and have puppies of her own. She will come into heat every six months.

But your female may not yet be old enough to take good care of puppies. And your family may not want any puppies. Then you must keep your dog away from male dogs when she comes into heat. Keep her away for three weeks after the bleeding starts. Otherwise males will sniff around her and mate with her.

Female dogs can have an operation called "spaying" that stops them from coming into heat and having puppies. Spaying is not a serious operation. If your family wants your dog to be spayed, she will have to stay in the animal hospital for only one night.

By the time your dog is one year old, a lot of things have happened to him. He has gotten shots and scoldings and shakings. Nobody liked his muddy feet or his puddles on the rug. But he has been a lot of fun, too. He has played with you, and learned tricks, and made you proud of him.

At one year old your puppy is grown up. He can have a birthday party. Maybe he has lost his ball. A new ball would be a good birthday present. Maybe he has grown out of his small bed. You could give him an old blanket to sleep on. And just this once, he could have real hamburger for his dinner. Shape it into a cake and bake it like a meatloaf. Decorate the cake with dog biscuits.

And what about you? It's a lot of work to raise a puppy. You should get a piece of meatloaf cake or some cookies. But maybe no one needs to blow out a candle and make a wish. Maybe your wish has already come true. You have just the dog you wanted, and he has you.

Index

DATE			

© THE BAKER & TAYLOR CO.